This Coloring Book Belongs To Queen:

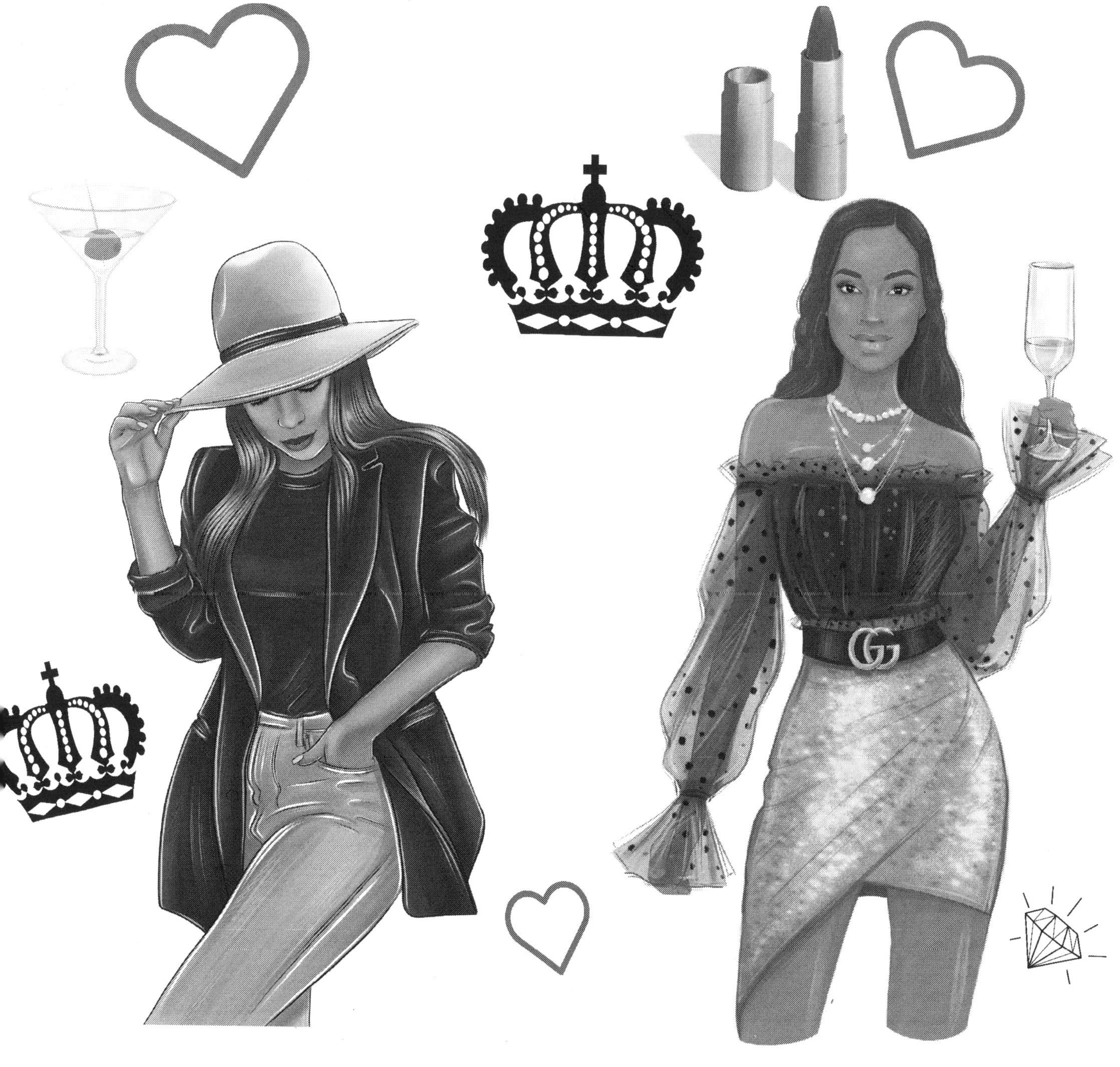

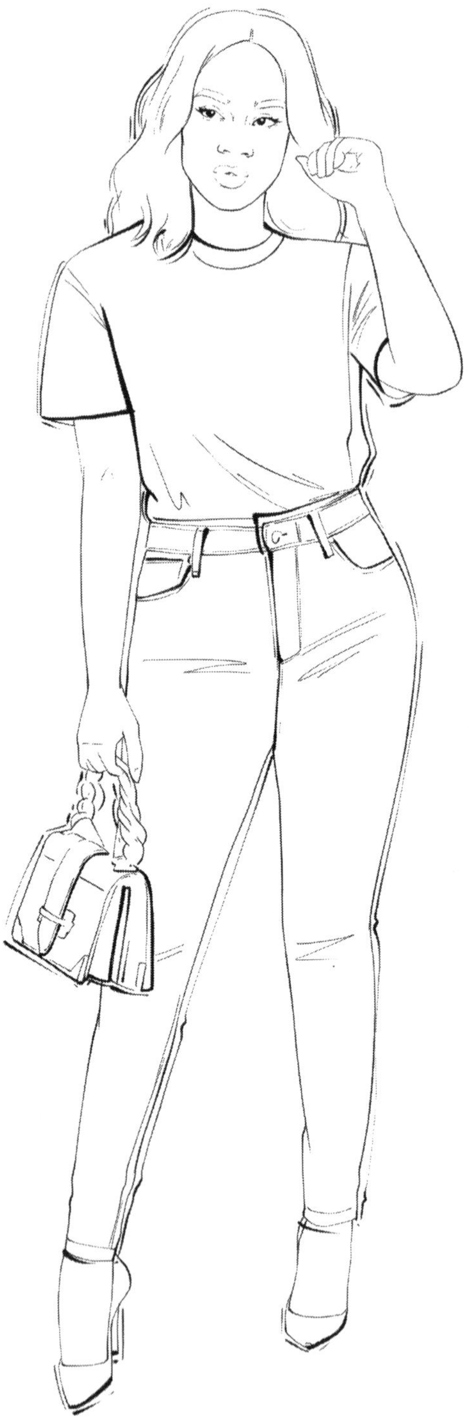

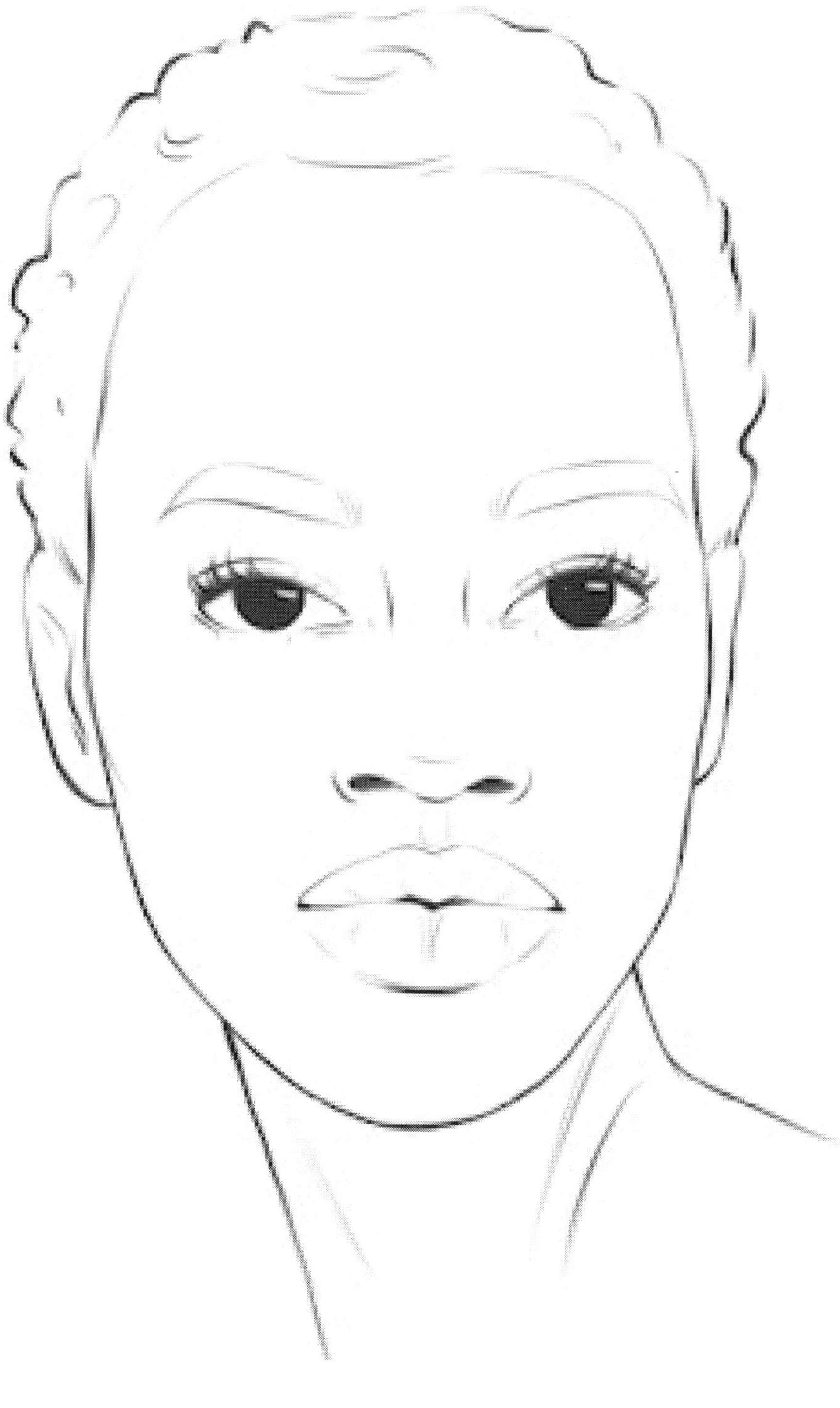

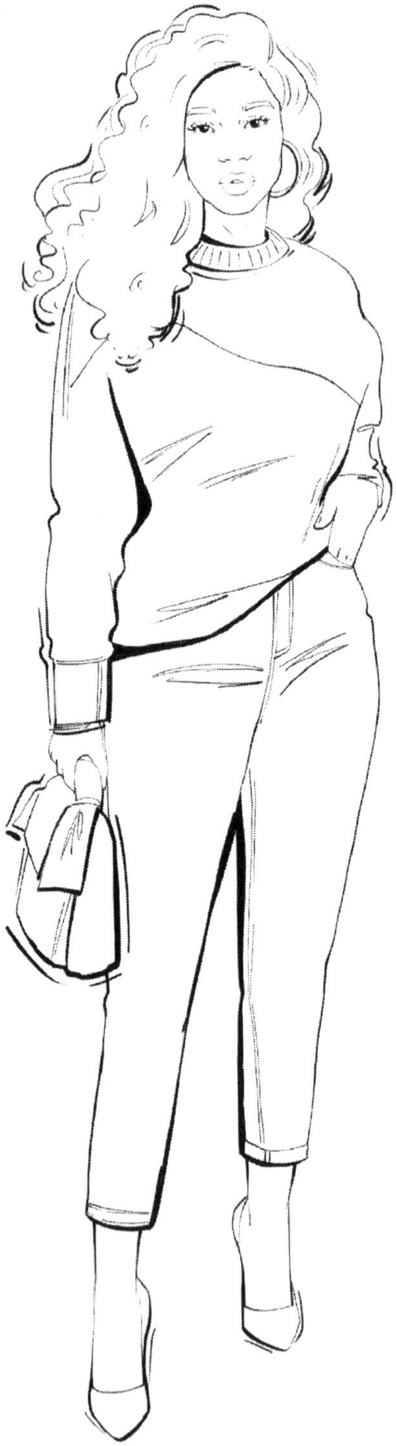

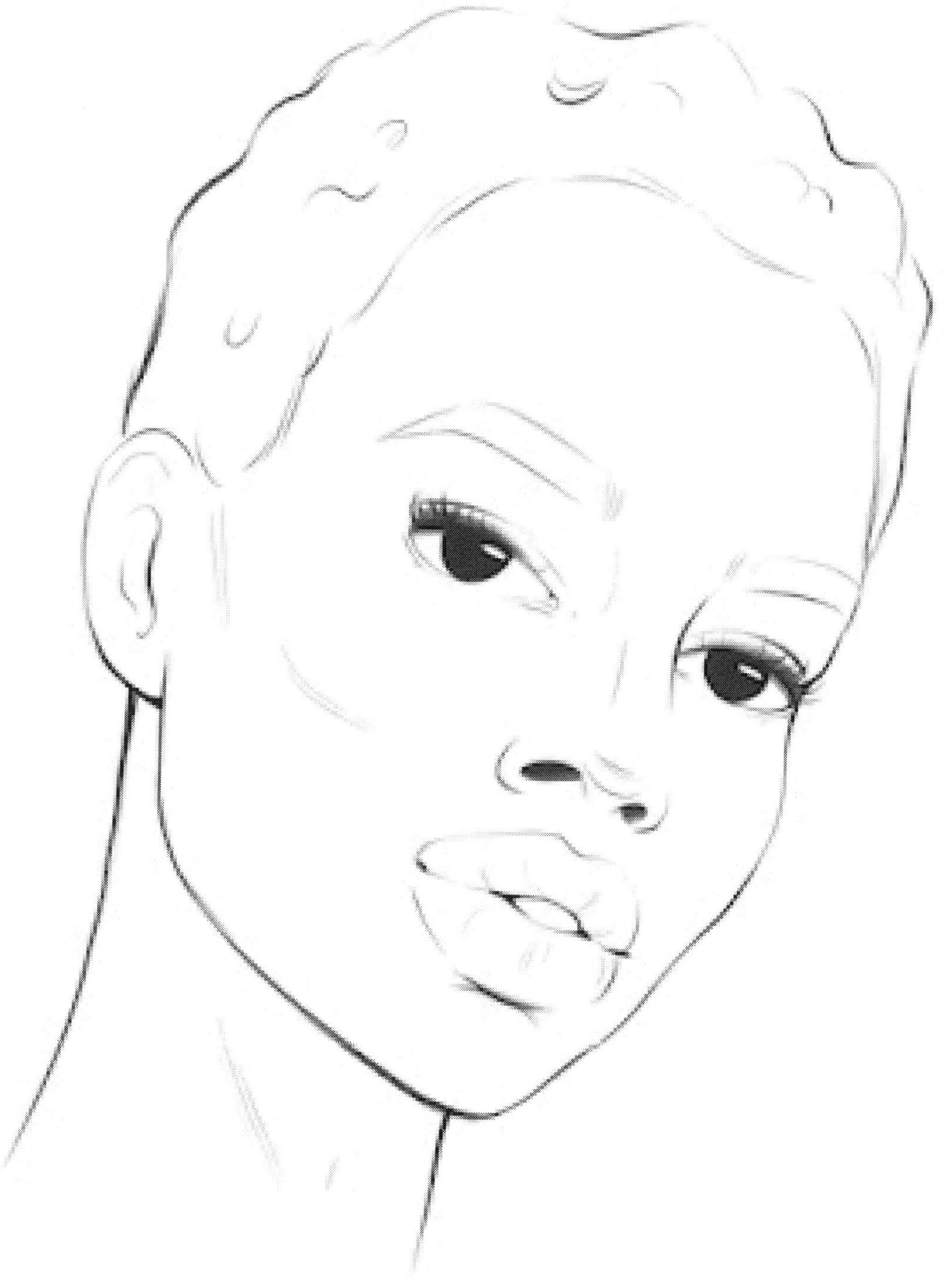

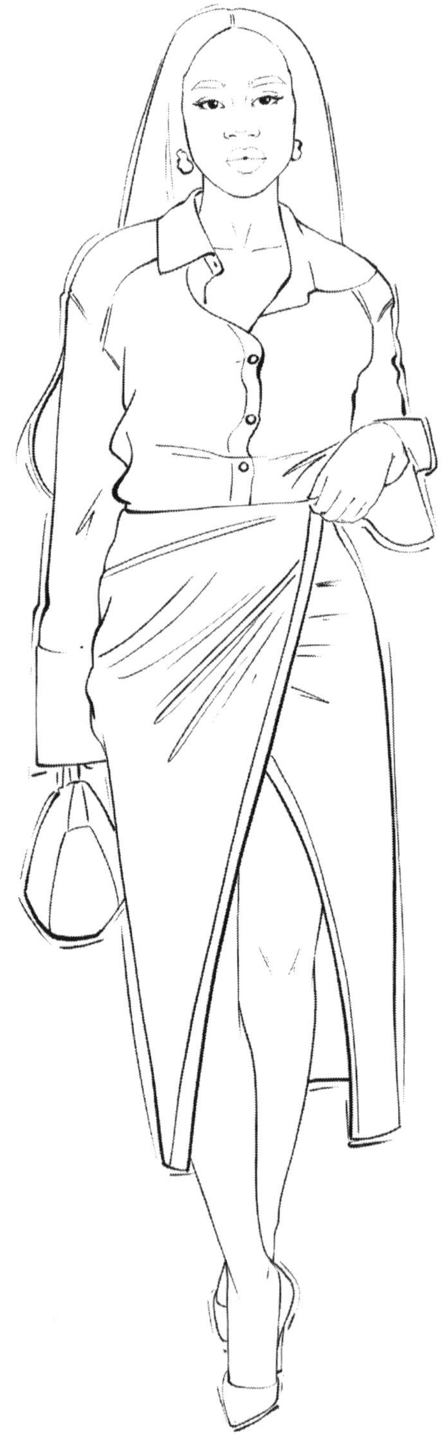

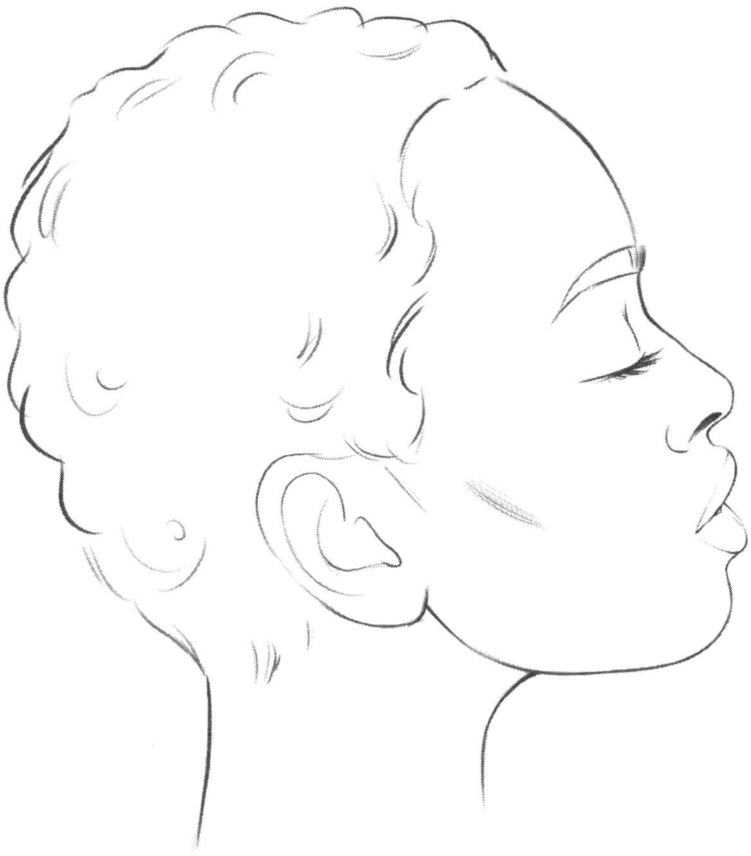

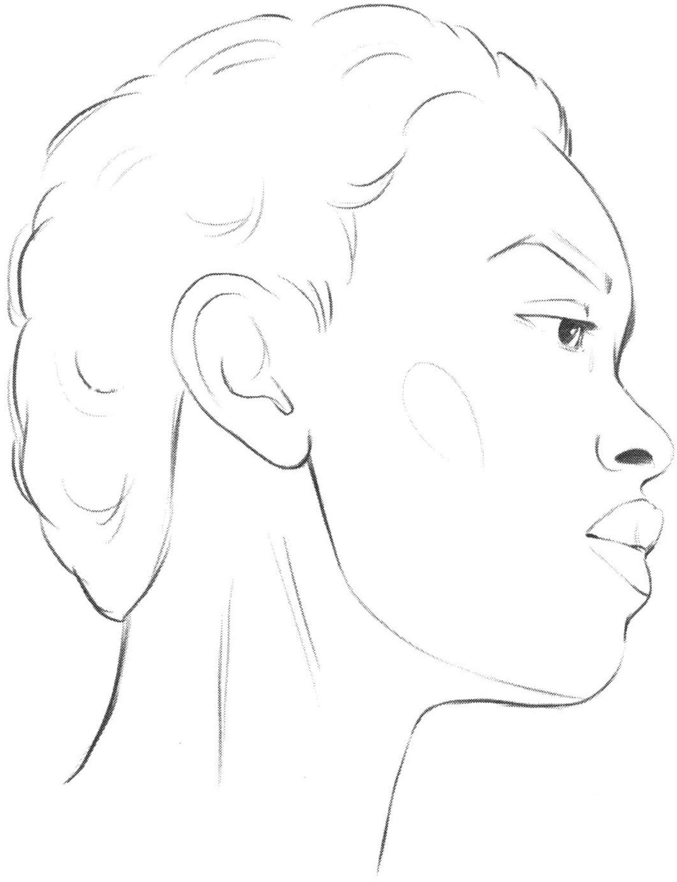

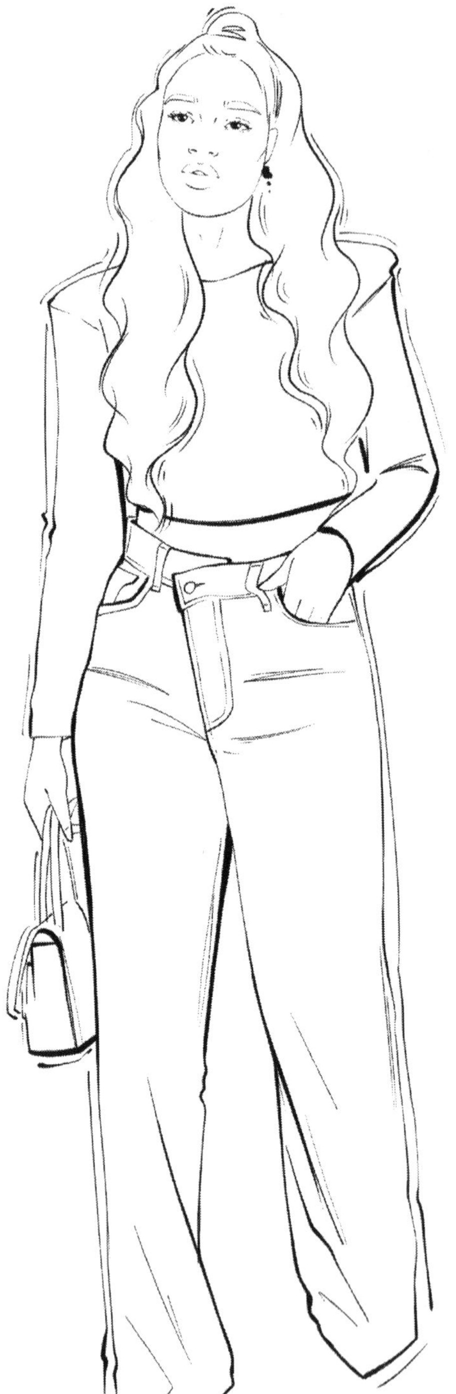

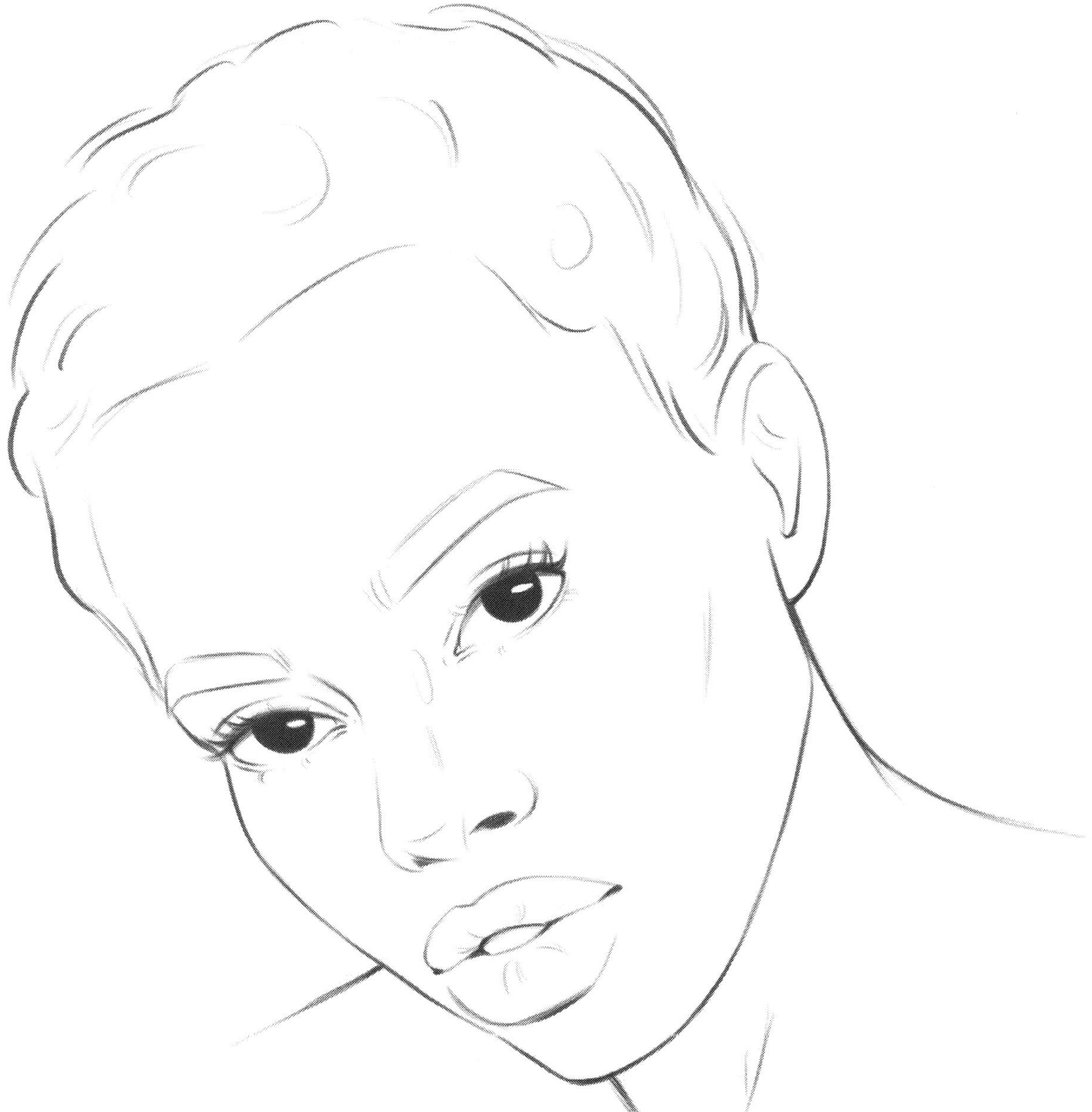

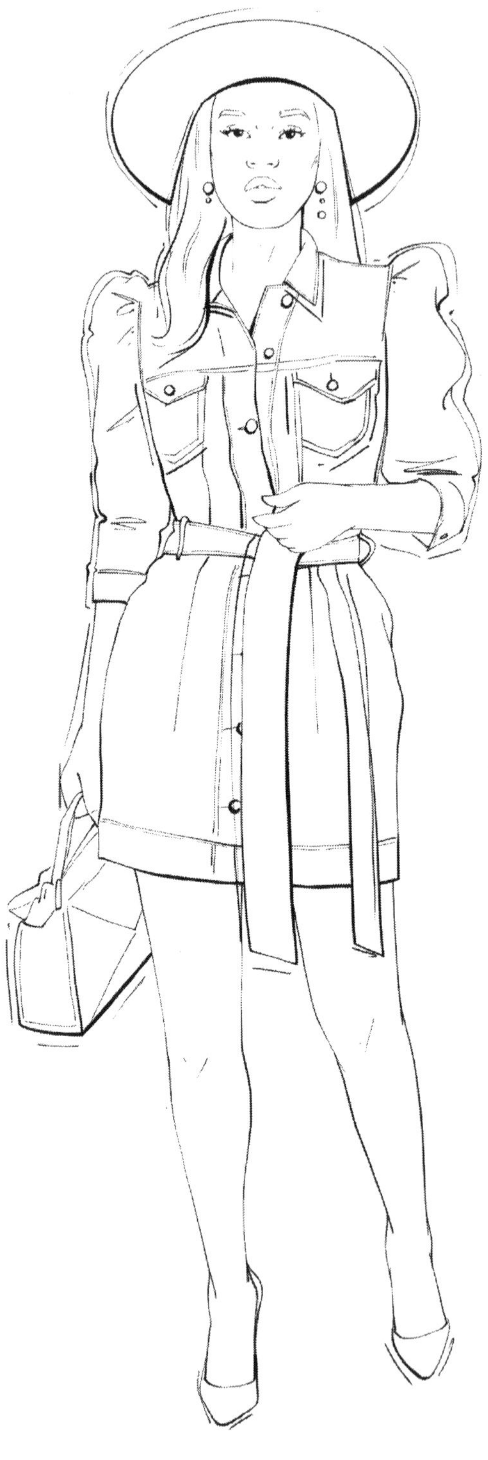

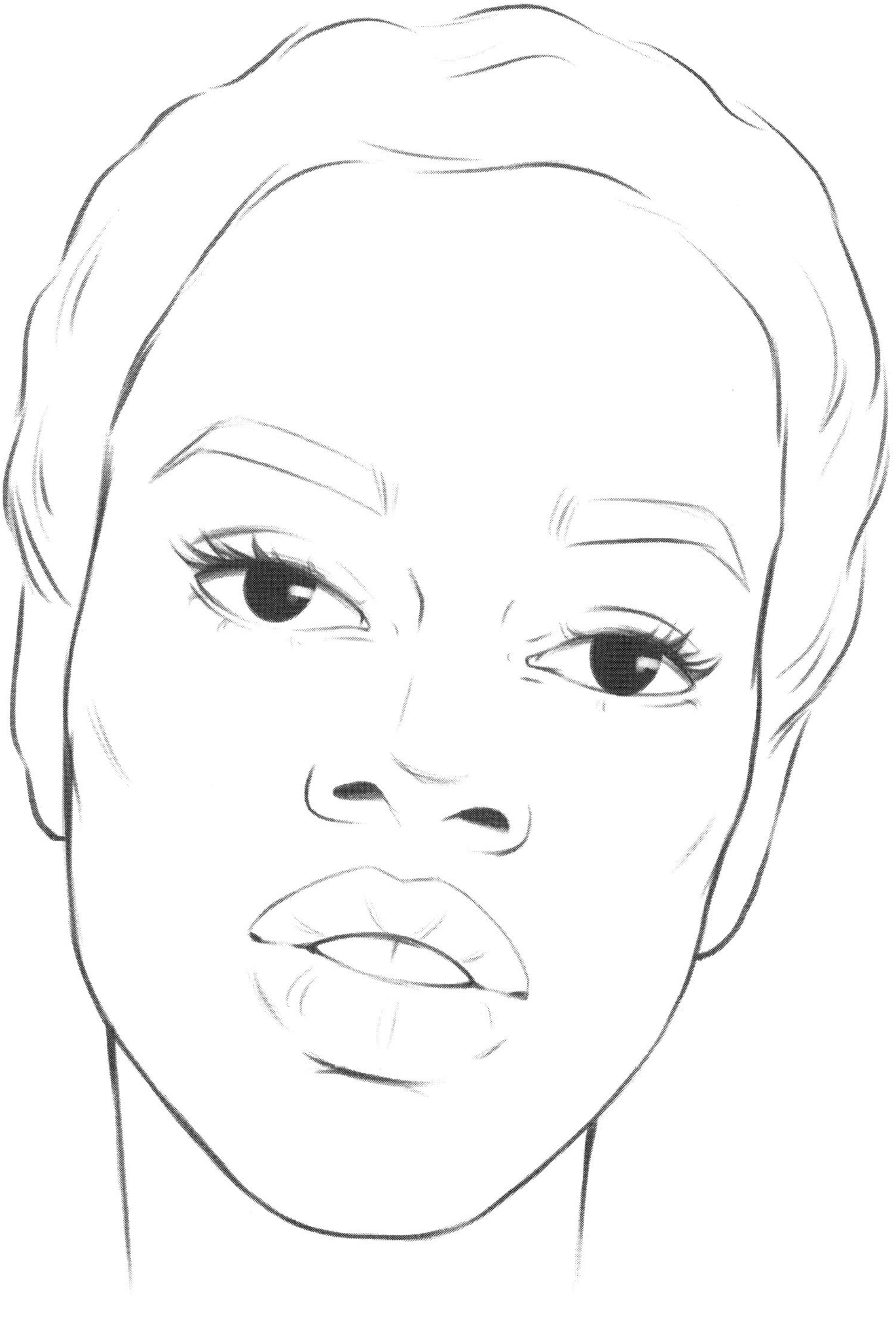

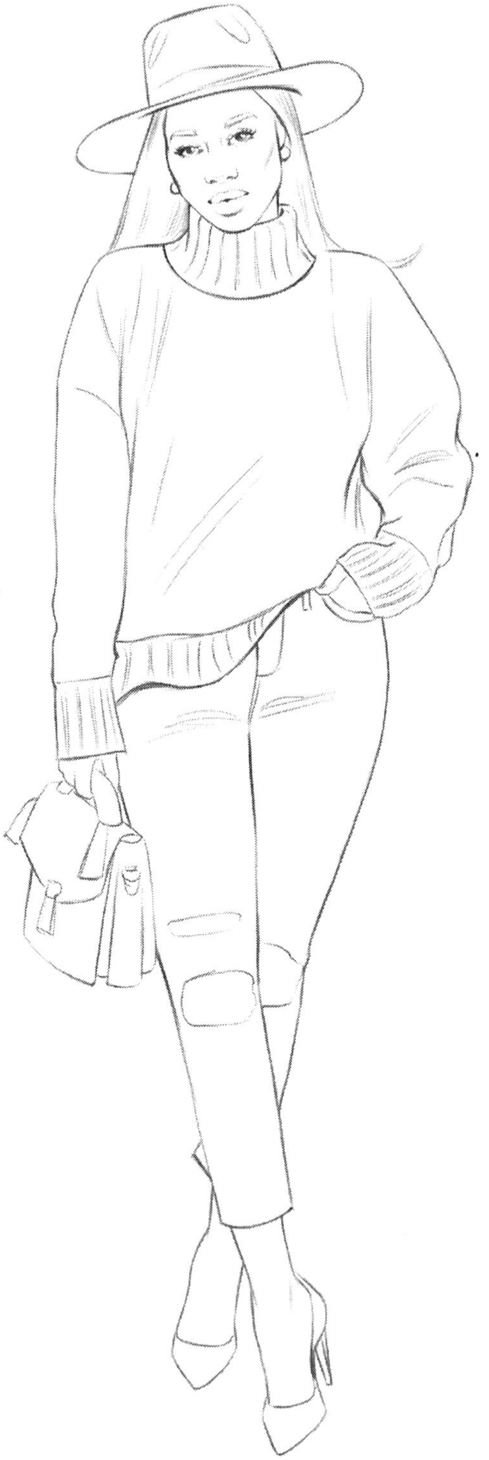

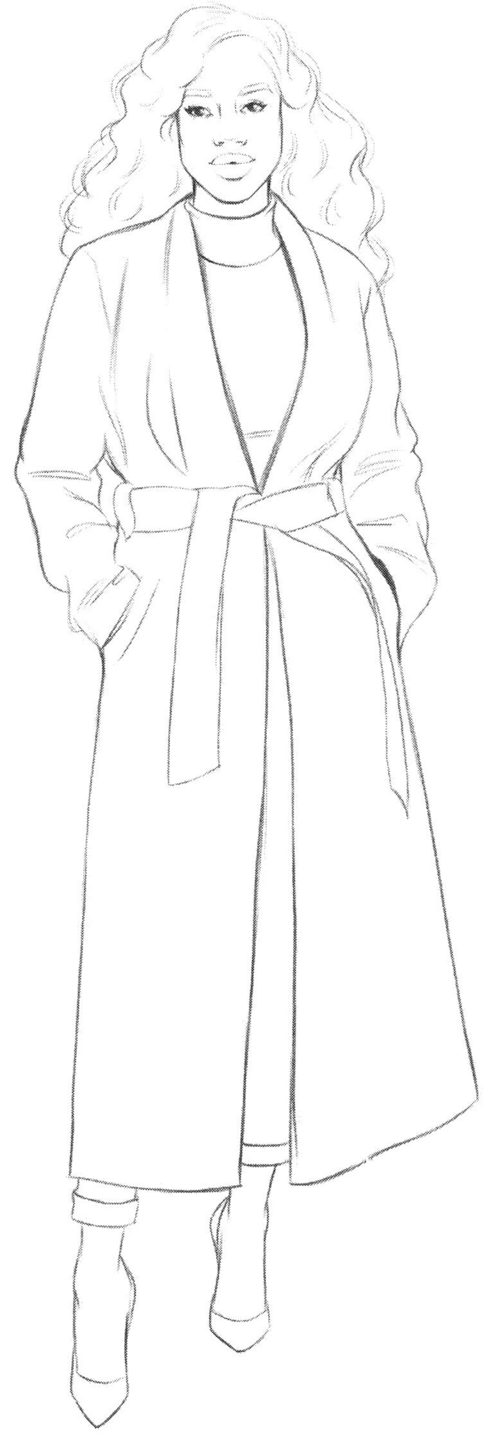

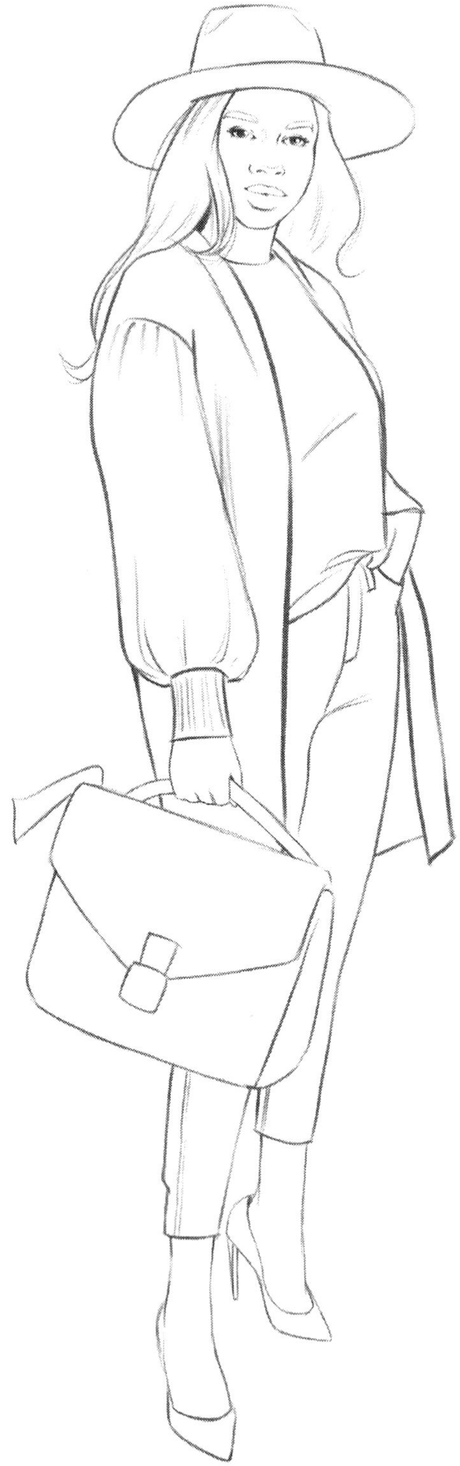

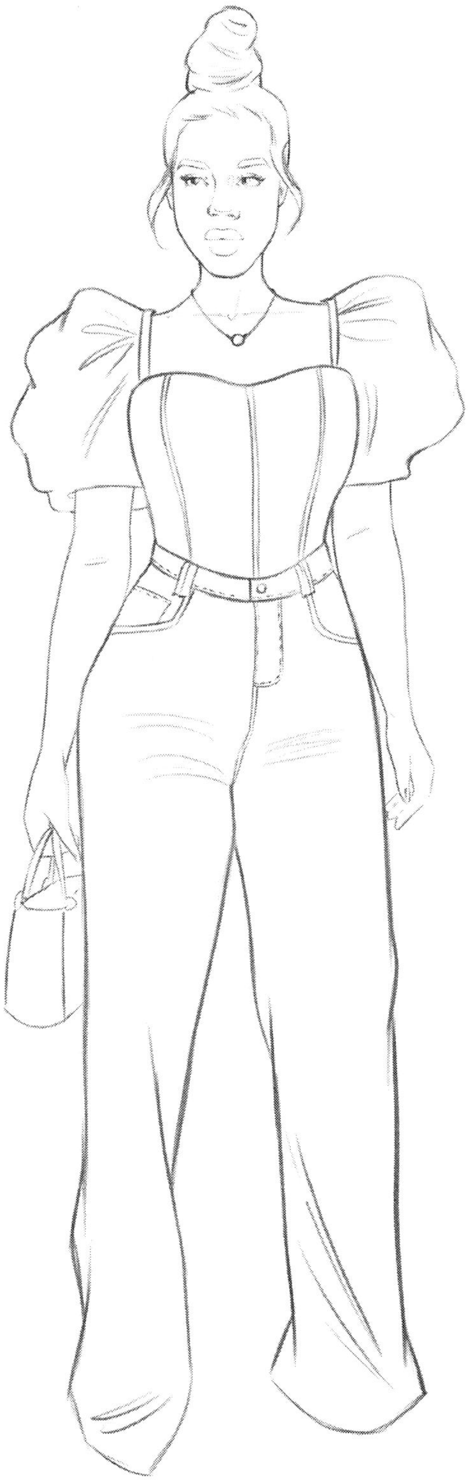

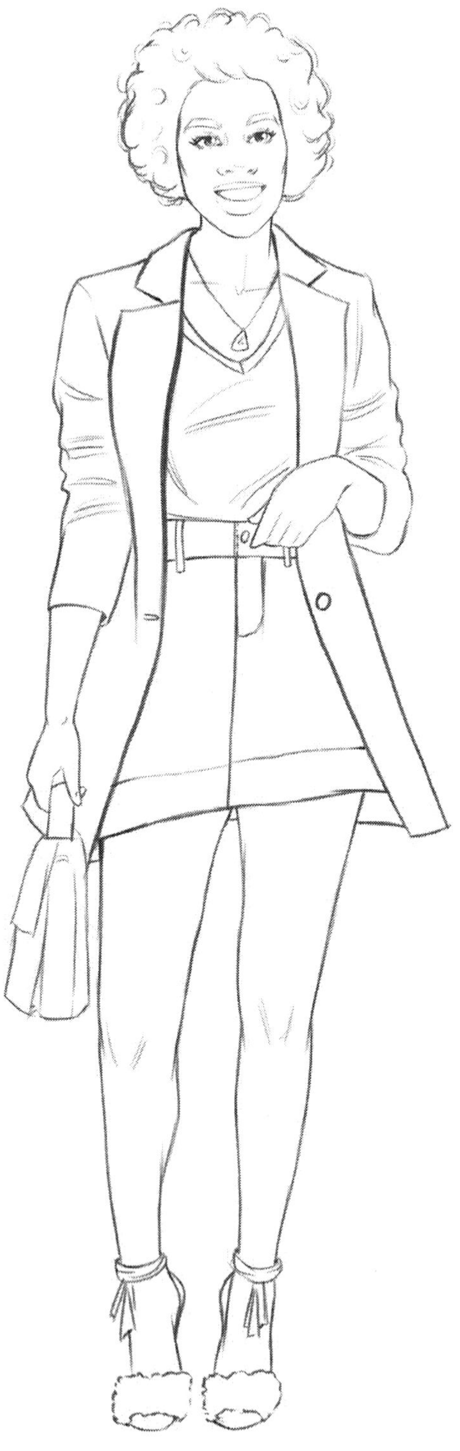

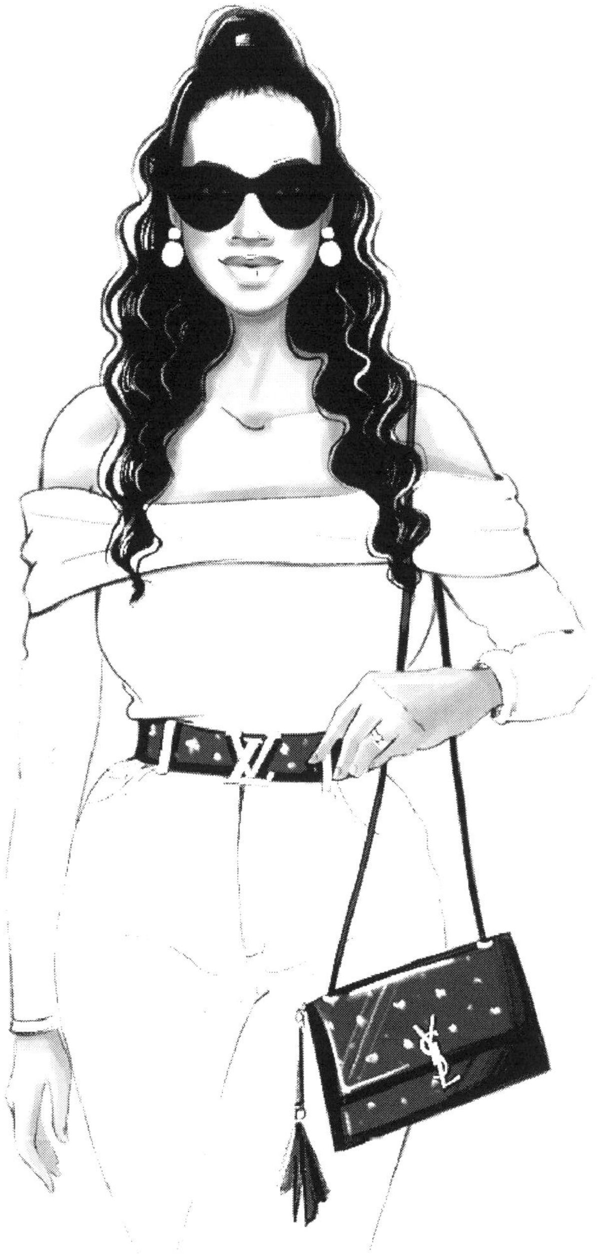

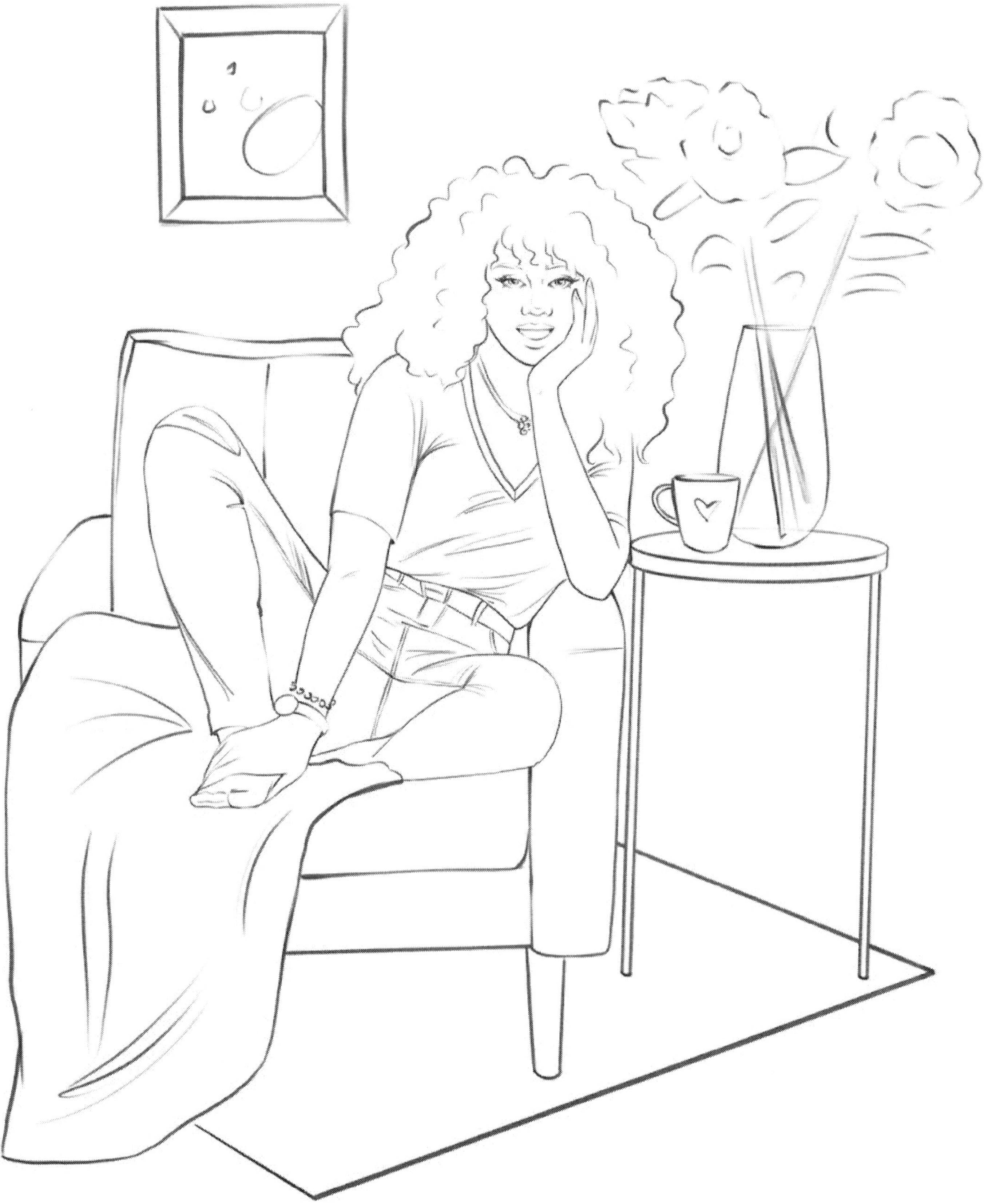

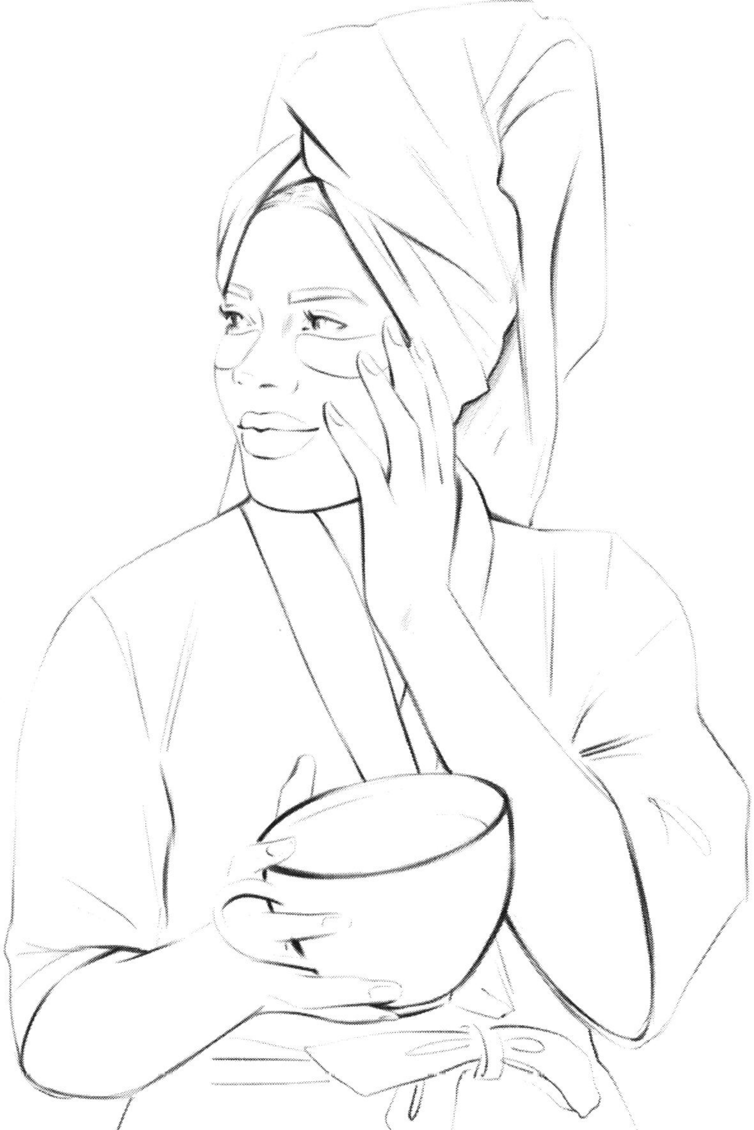

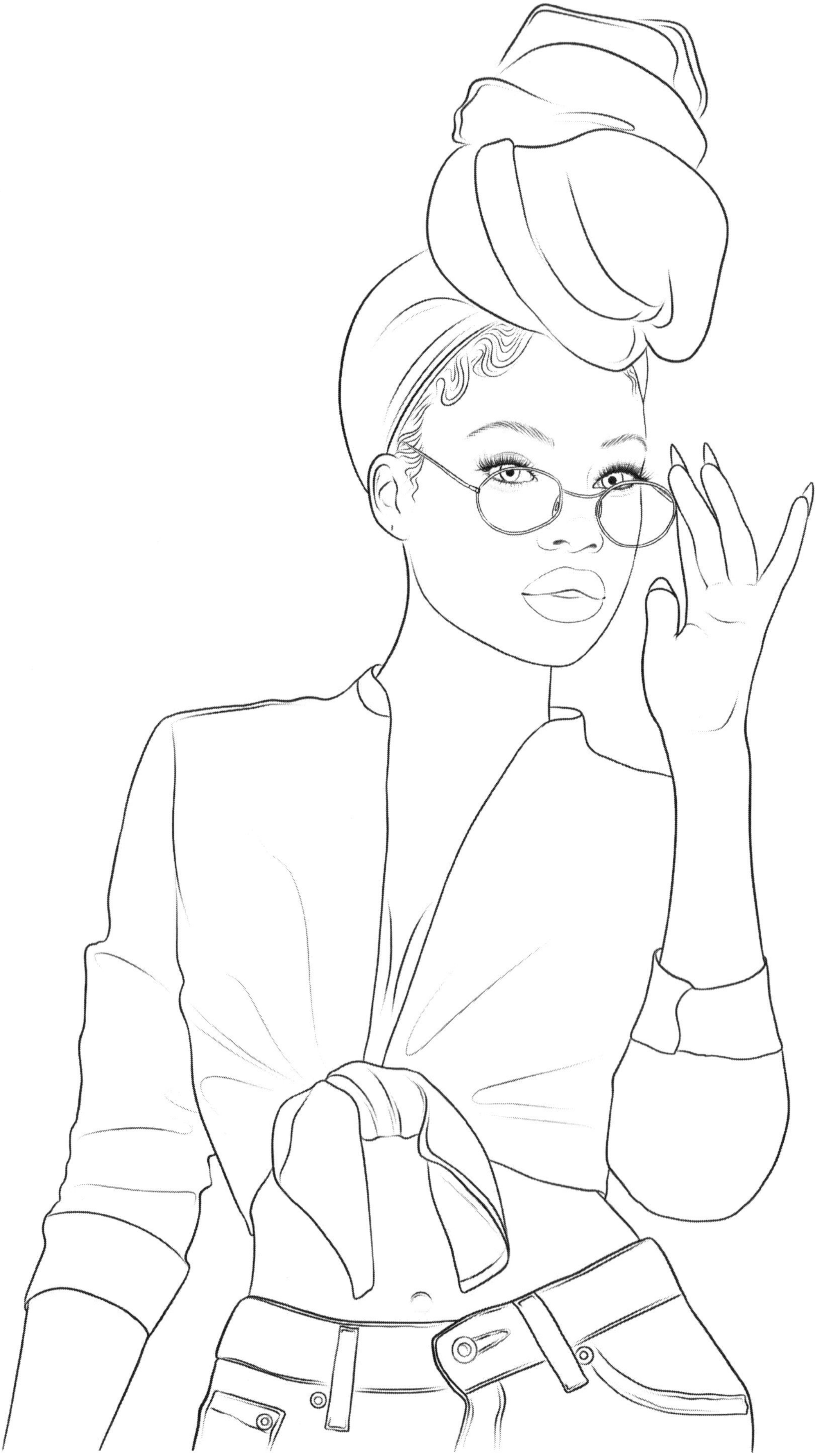

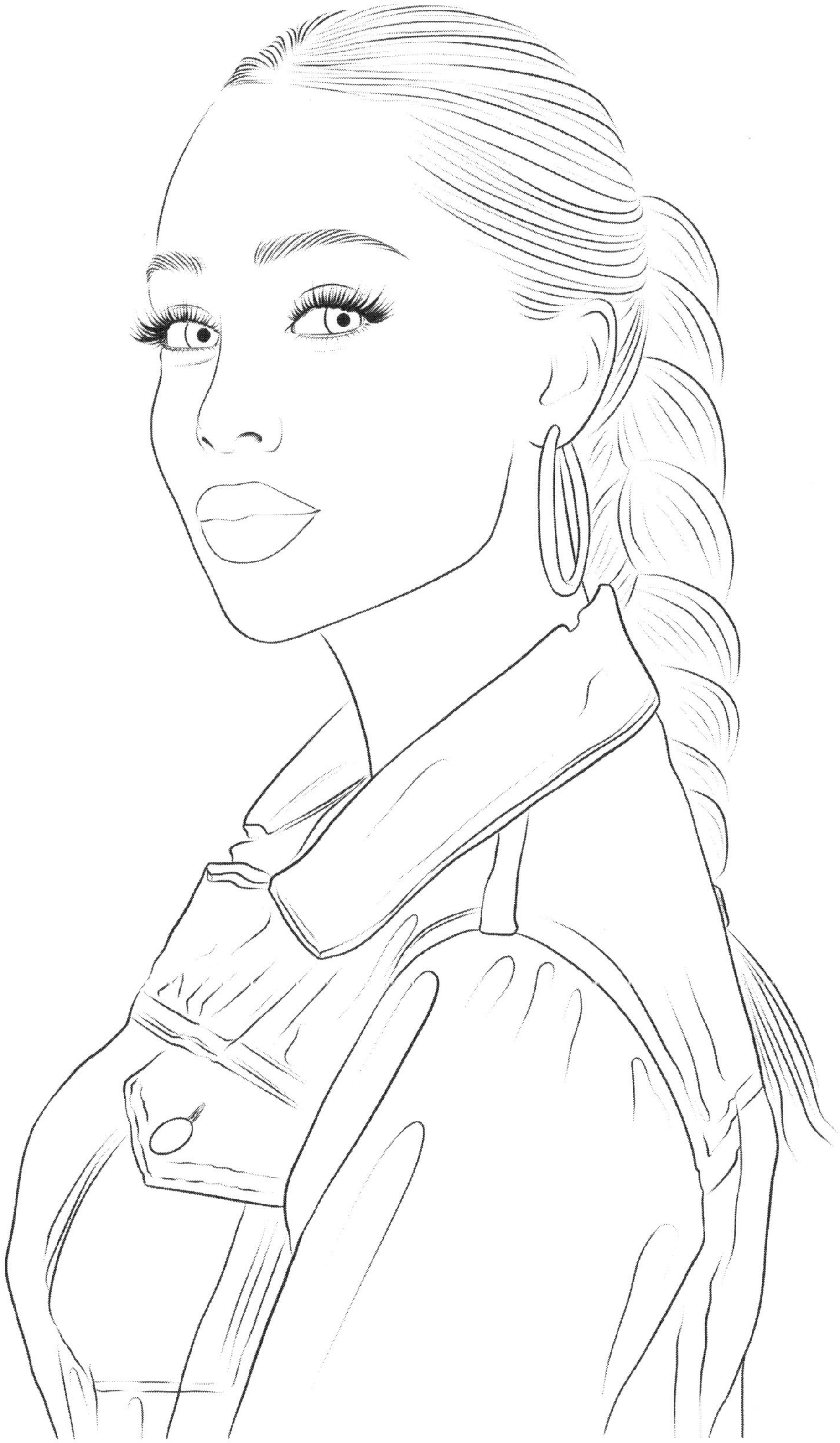

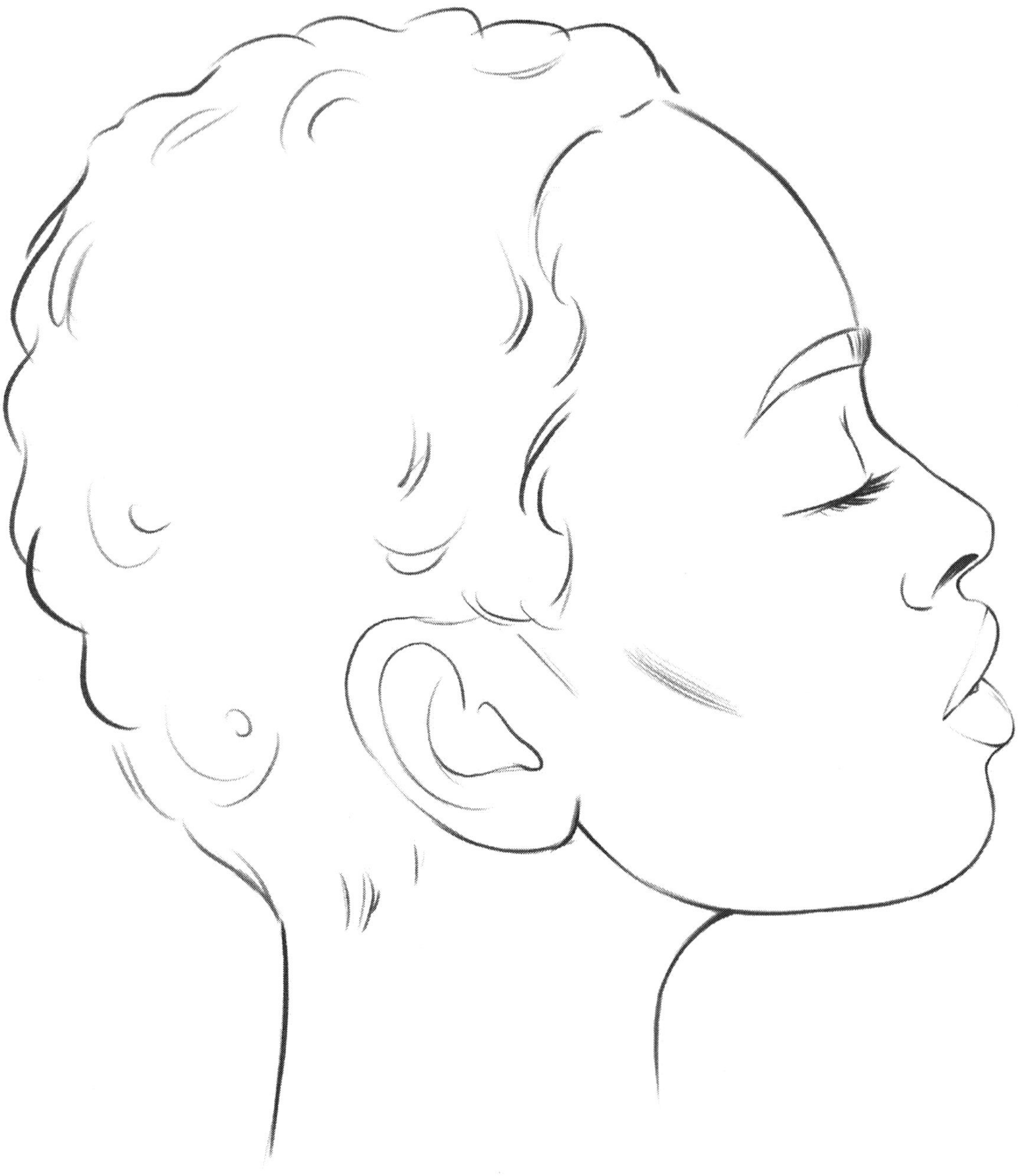

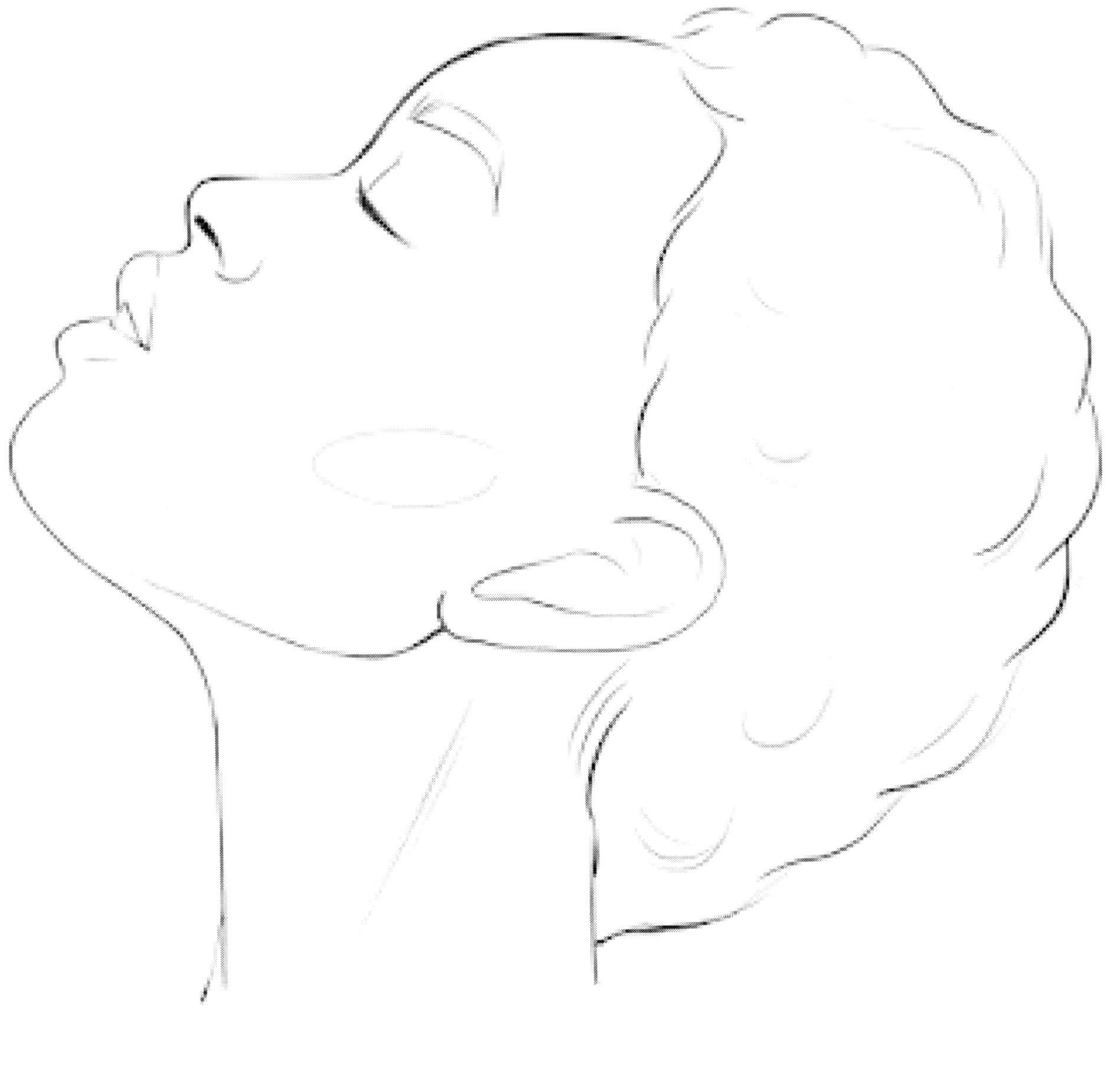

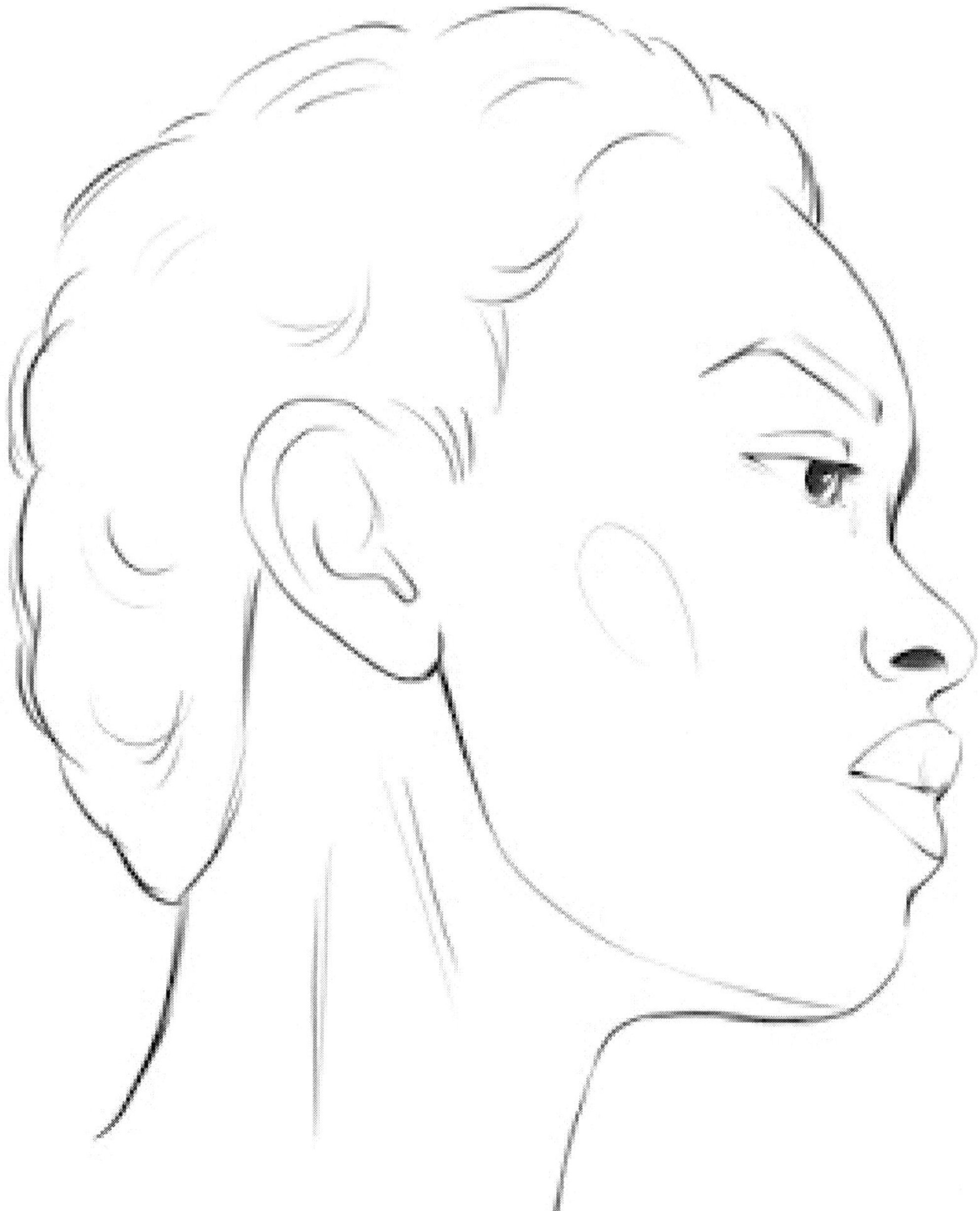

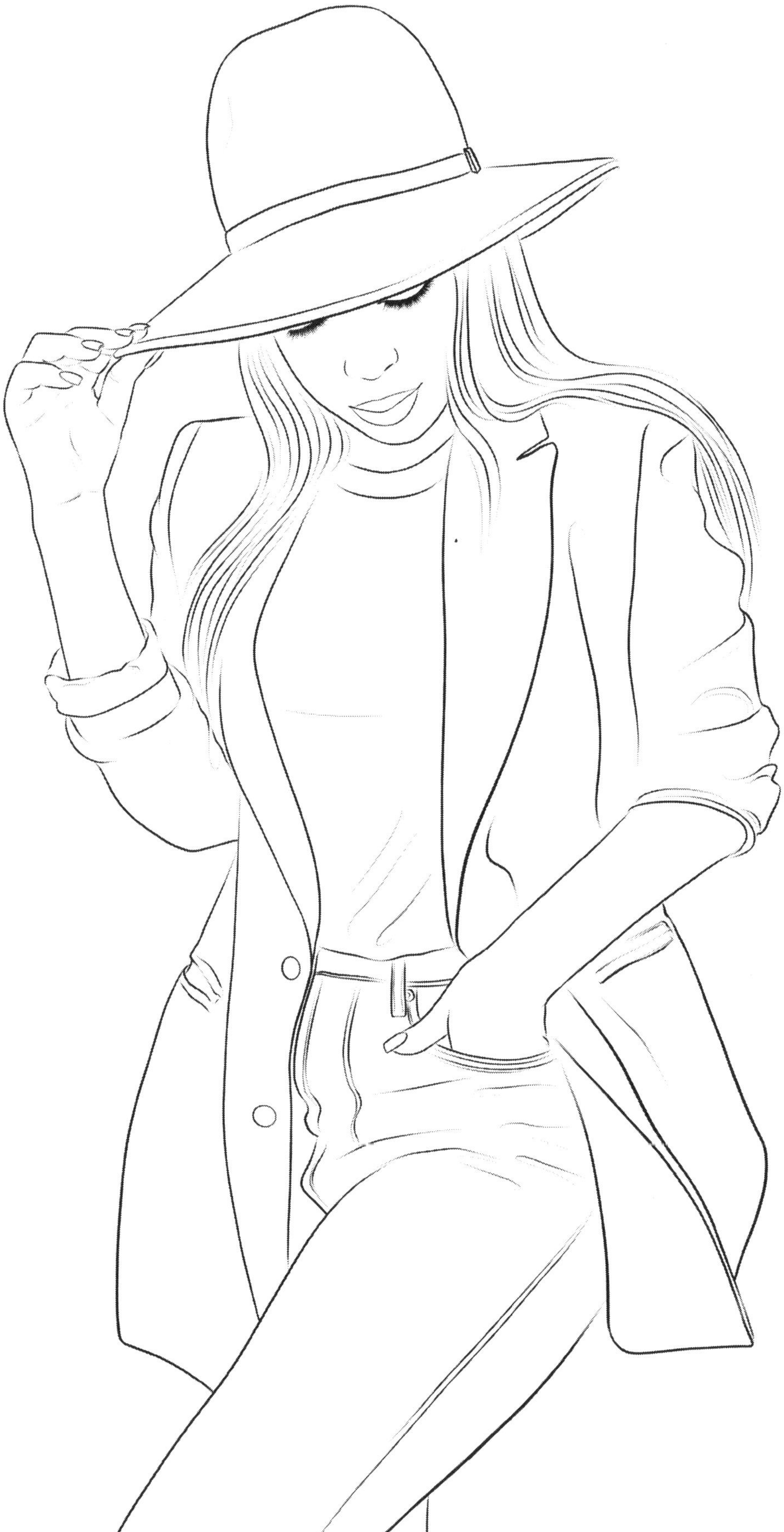

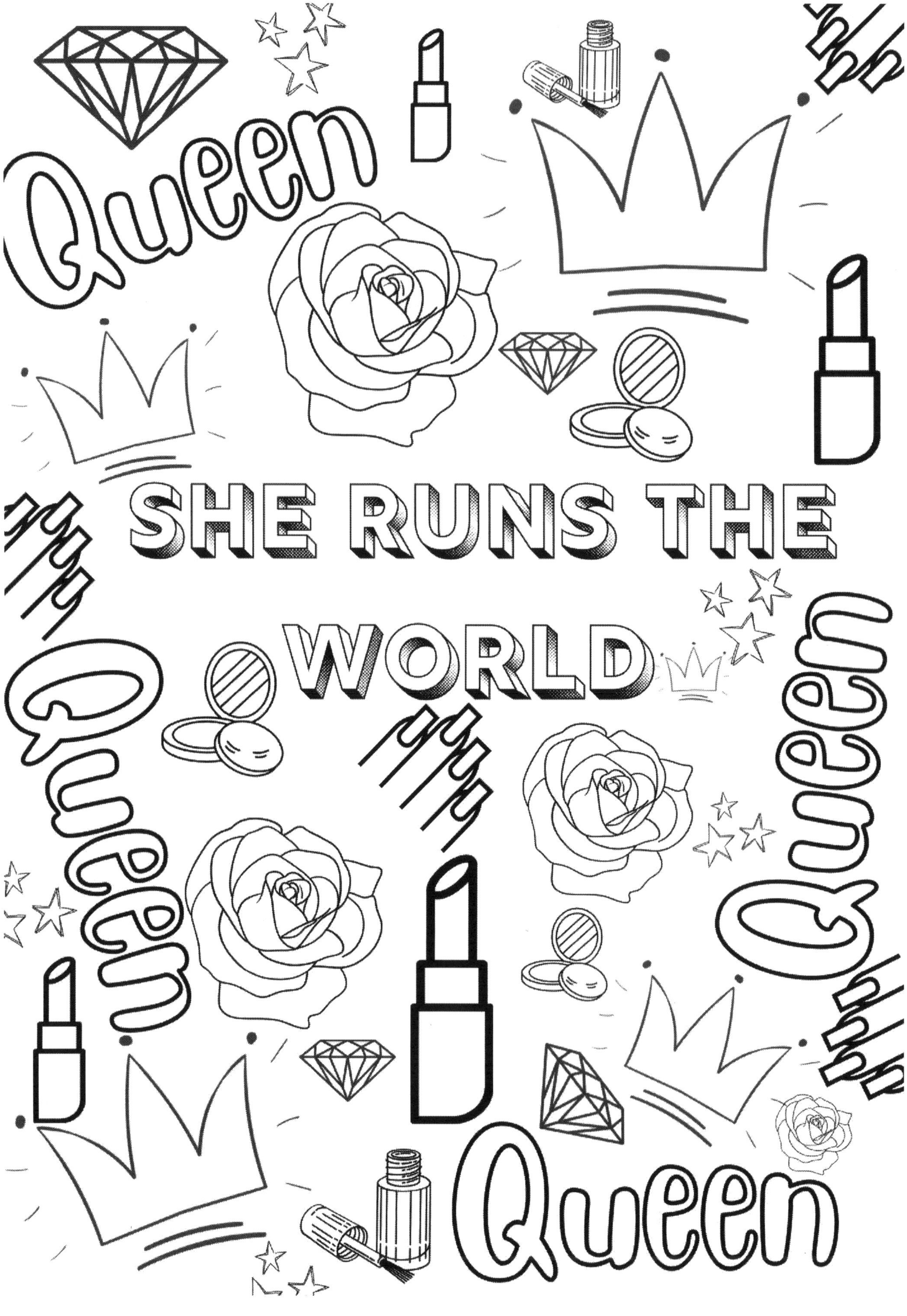
Queen
SHE RUNS THE
WORLD
Queen
Queen
Queen

Made in the USA
Middletown, DE
23 June 2023

33254635R00015